How to Create Language Experts With
Literary Terms

Codi Hrouda and Emma McInerney
with Lyle Lee Jenkins

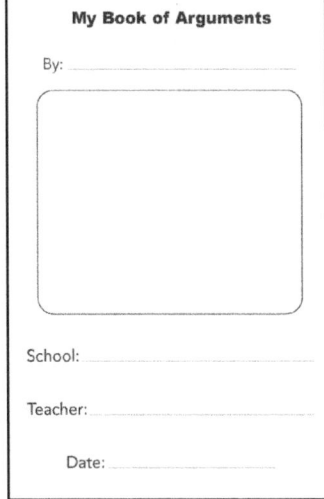

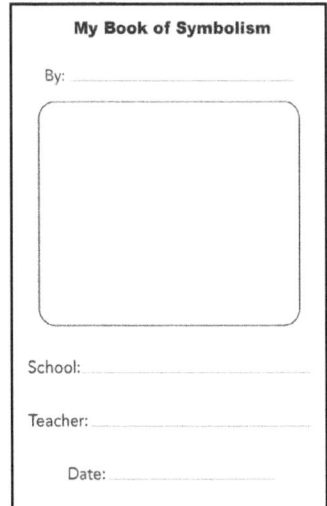

Perfect School Collection™

To contact the authors regarding keynotes, workshops or bulk orders, visit LtoJ.net/Contact

ISBN: 978-1-956457-71-1

Book Design & Graphics: Christy Courtright, Christy's Customs LLC
Quality Assurance Manager: Kelly Lippert
Publishing Consultant: Martha Bullen, Bullen Publishing Services
Distribution Coordinator: Maggie McLaughlin

Printed in the United States of America

The Perfect School Collection™

How to Create a Perfect School by Lyle Lee Jenkins

How to Create a Perfect Home School by Lyle Lee Jenkins and Kelly Hawkinson Lippert

Perfect School Collection™ Resources

How to Create Math Experts series by Peggy McLean and Lyle Lee Jenkins

How to Create Math Experts with Fluency Quizzes by Peggy McLean and Lyle Lee Jenkins

How to Create Math Experts with Math Standards Quizzes by Peggy McLean, Laura Hayes and Lyle Lee Jenkins

How to Create a Math Foundation for Future Math Experts by Lyle Lee Jenkins

How to Create Bible Experts: Genesis to Revelation by Richard Douglas Junior Jenkins with Lyle Lee Jenkins

Early Readers

Bible Patterns for Young Readers series by Lyle Lee Jenkins

Aesop Patterns for Young Readers series by Lyle Lee Jenkins

Young Authors

Wordless Books for Young Authors series by Jim Chansler and Lyle Lee Jenkins

Special Project

All About Henry: Rich Widower of Savannah Valley by Lyle Lee Jenkins

CONTENTS

INTRODUCTION

The philosophy behind these booklets is that they are student-led, and elementary (K - 6) standards driven. In other words, students can independently complete much of the materials they are expected to learn in school with occasional pre-teaching.

The booklets are designed with a left-brain/right-brain balance. The back cover is a right-brain activity and the inside pages are clearly left-brain. The page prior to each grade level gives parents and teachers background knowledge and suggestions to successfully support their students and children through the booklets.

In order to create and assemble the booklets, parents and teachers can scan the QR code provided at the end of the book to download digital copies. To ensure proper printing, please utilize double sided printing and set your printer to "flip" on the short edge. The front page will be the front and back cover of the booklet. We have also included some bonus booklets within this series to support additional literary term exploration.

Enjoy,

Codi Hrouda, Emma McInerney and Lyle Lee Jenkins

GRADE 6
BOOKLET DIRECTIONS

My Book of Greek Roots:
Students may need to be pre-taught root words and given examples.

My Book of Inferential Questions:
Students will need access to a literary chapter book of their choosing.

My Book of Breaking Down a Plot to Identify Theme:
Students will need access to a literary chapter book of their choosing.

My Book of Multicultural Perspectives:
Students will need access to a historical fiction book with multiple cultural perspectives.

Some books we suggest:
Refugee by Alan Gratz
Ground Zero by Alan Gratz
Towers Falling by Jewell Parker Rhodes

My Book of Central Ideas:
Students may need to be pre-taught central idea. Central idea is the secondary level term for main idea. The students will have prior knowledge of main idea from previous booklets. Access to a non-fiction book and coloring supplies will be needed for this booklet.

My Book of Arguments:
Students will need access to an opinion article on a topic of their choosing.

My Book of Allusions:
Students may need to be taught beforehand about allusion and given examples.

My Book of Puns:
Students may need to be pre-taught puns and given examples. A variety of text such as: articles, song lyrics, comic books will be needed for this booklet.

My Book of Symbolism:
Students may need to be pre-taught symbolism and given examples. Access to their favorite animated movie and coloring supplies will be needed for this booklet.

Student booklets are available via the QR code at the end of the book

Research more Greek roots. Then choose one to create a diagram that displays the root word with all the possible prefixes and suffixes that can be applied.

My Book of Greek Roots

By: _____

School: _____

Teacher: _____

Date: _____

Greek Roots - a word with a Greek origin that does not have a prefix or suffix, but one can be added to change the meaning of the word.
Example: root - **biblio**, **biblio**graphy

Match the following Greek roots with their meanings

Auto
(autobiography, automatic)

A. Life

Bio
(biography, biology)

B. Water

Meter
(thermometer, speedometer)

C. People

Dem
(democracy, demographics)

D. Write

Hydro
(hydrant, hydroflask)

E. Self

Graph
(autography, calligraphy)

F. Measure

List as many related words as you can find for each Greek root:

dec	gram
phon	micro

Student booklets are available via the QR code at the end of the book

Write an interview for a character of a book you've read. Ask multiple inferential questions and answer these questions as to how you think the character would respond.

_____

_____

_____

_____

_____

_____

_____

_____

_____

My Book of Inferential Questions

By: _____

School: _____

Teacher: _____

Date: _____

Inferential Questions - questions whose answers are not found directly in the text. To answer these questions, the reader has to look for clues in the text and connect them with what they already know in order to figure out what the author is saying.

Read a chapter book and after every few chapters, stop to write and answer inferential questions.

_____
Book Title

Chapter	Inferential Question(s)	Answer(s)

Student booklets are available via the QR code at the end of the book

Pick two of your favorite songs. Use the lyrics to help you identify the implied themes.

_____
First Song Title

Implied Theme:

_____

_____

_____

_____
Second Song Title

Implied Theme:

_____

_____

_____

My Book of Breaking Down a Plot to Identify Theme

By: _____

School: _____

Teacher: _____

Date: _____

Read a literary book and complete the plot diagram below describing the important details. Be sure to label the elements of plot. Then use the completed plot diagram to help you identify the implied theme of the story.

In this story, the implied theme is _____

_____

_____

Student booklets are available via the QR code at the end of the book

Research a current event (example: climate change) form two different cultural perspectives and complete the Venn Diagram.

My Book of Multicultural Perspectives

By: _____

_____ Current Event

Culture 1

Same

Culture 2

School: _____

Teacher: _____

Date: _____

Read a historical fiction book with multiple cultural perspectives. Then complete the Venn Diagram below.

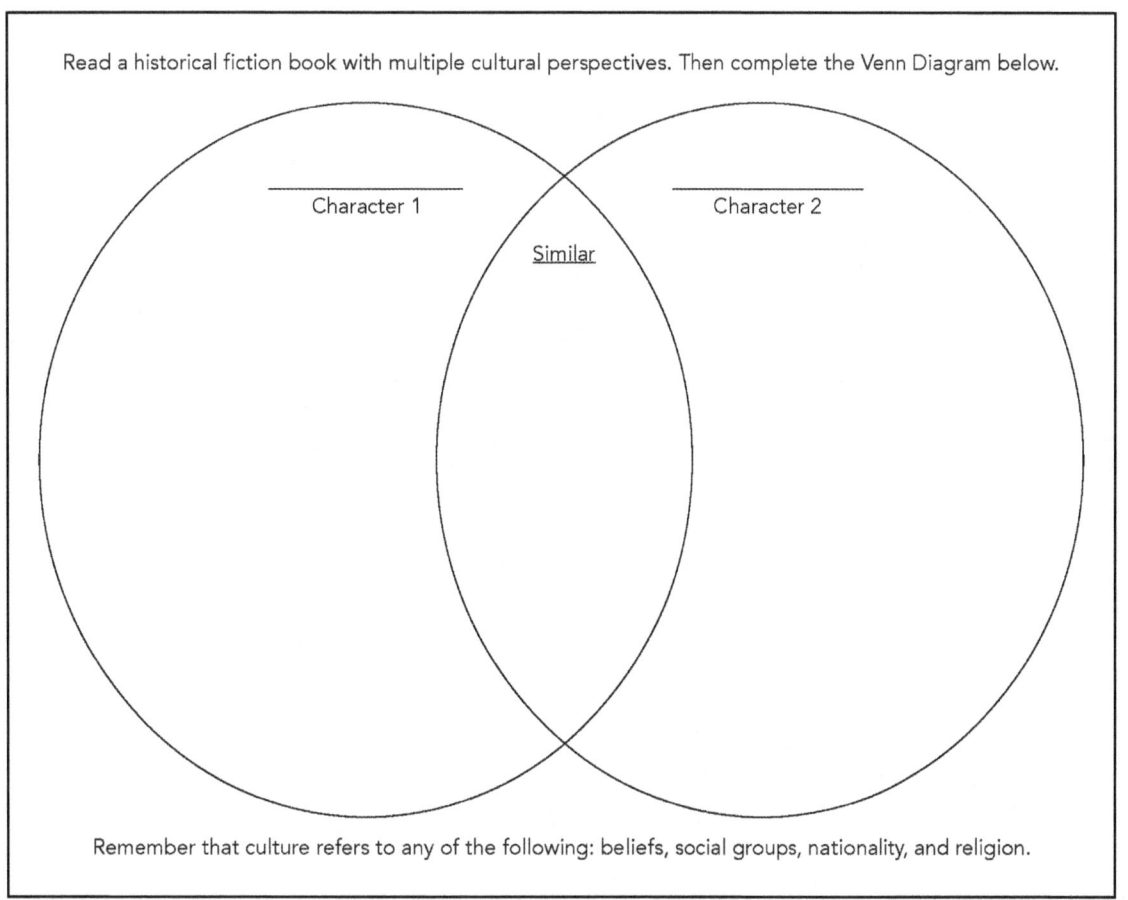

_____ Character 1

Similar

_____ Character 2

Remember that culture refers to any of the following: beliefs, social groups, nationality, and religion.

Student booklets are available via the QR code at the end of the book

Create a slogan for the text you completed on the inside pages.

My Book of Central Ideas

By: _____

School: _____

Teacher: _____

Date: _____

Central Idea - the main focus of a text.

Read a non-fiction text and complete the graphic organizer below to help you identify the central idea.

Step 1

Topic:

Remember to look at text features to help you!

Step 2

Big Idea 1:

Big Idea 2:

Big Idea 3:

Step 3

Central Idea:

Student booklets are available via the QR code at the end of the book

Create your own argument on a current topic

My Book of Arguments

_____
Topic

By: _____

My opinion:

_____
_____
_____

Biases	Actual Facts

School: _____

Teacher: _____

Date: _____

Bias - to favor some ideas or people over others.

Read an opinion article on a topic of your choice, Complete the chart below to show how the author defends their opinions by using actual facts and biases for their overall argument.

_____
Topic

Author's opinion:

_____
_____

Biases	Actual Facts

Create multiple allusions of your own:

My Book of Allusions

By: _____

School: _____

Teacher: _____

Date: _____

Allusion - a reference within a literary text to a person, place, event, or to another work of literature. Example: Peanut butter is my "achilles heel". The term "achilles heel" comes from Greek mythology meaning something's weakness.

Read the following statements and identify what it's alluding to:

She felt like she had won a golden ticket.

_____

He's a real Einstein.

_____

Sally told her crying sister to let it go.

_____

If I'm not home by midnight, my car will turn into a pumpkin.

_____

A lot of allusions come from Greek mythology. Research these modern day allusions and list their connections below.

Modern Day	Greek Mythology

Create multiple puns of your own.

My Book of Puns

By: _____

School: _____

Teacher: _____

Date: _____

Puns - a play on words, that is used as a comical relief within a text.
Example: I'm so **board** I really wish something fun **wood** come along.

Read each pun and underline the word(s) or phrase(s) that represents play on word. Then read it to a family member and see if they get it.

1. Past, present, and future walked into the room. It was tense.

2. I work as a baker because I knead dough.

3. To write with a broken pencil is pointless.

4. I couldn't figure out how to buckle my seatbelt. Then it clicked!

Find puns within a variety of text (songs, comic strips, graphic novels, etc.) and copy them down.

Text	Pun
_____	_____
_____	_____
_____	_____
_____	_____
_____	_____
_____	_____
_____	_____
_____	_____

Draw a picture with multiple symbols that represent your life.

My Book of Symbolism

By: _____

School: _____

Teacher: _____

Date: _____

Symbolism - when a word is used to mean or represent something other than its typical definition, to help authors communicate their messages to readers.
Example: **Rose** is often used to represent **love**.

Match each example of symbolism to what it represents:

Four Leaf Clover   A. Luck

Broken Mirror   B. Doom

Dove   C. Evilness

Snake   D.   Life or Purity

Dark Clouds   E. Bad Luck

Watch your favorite animated movie and try to identify the hidden symbols within the movie.

_____
Movie Title

Symbolism	Represents

CONTINUE CREATING LITERARY EXPERTS

BONUS BOOKLETS

A quick internet search for literary terms brings up hundreds of words. In addition, there are many topics to study as students gain more meaning from language and increase their writing skills.

Thus, the following blank pages are designed for students to write additional booklets about literary terms not included in *How to Create Language Experts with Literary Terms*. After selecting a new term, students select the format that best fits the task of writing about the literary term or concept.

There are times when children become so engrossed with a particular term that they want to make their booklet larger. These blank pages can also be used to add to existing booklets included in *How to Create Language Experts with Literary Terms*.

Student booklets are available via the QR code at the end of the book

My Book of _____

By: _____

School: _____

Teacher: _____

Date: _____

_____
Title of Book 1

_____
Title of Book 2

Student booklets are available via the QR code at the end of the book

My art:

Student booklets are available via the QR code at the end of the book

Book 1 Title: _____   Book 2 Title: _____

Book Title

Book Title

Student booklets are available via the QR code at the end of the book

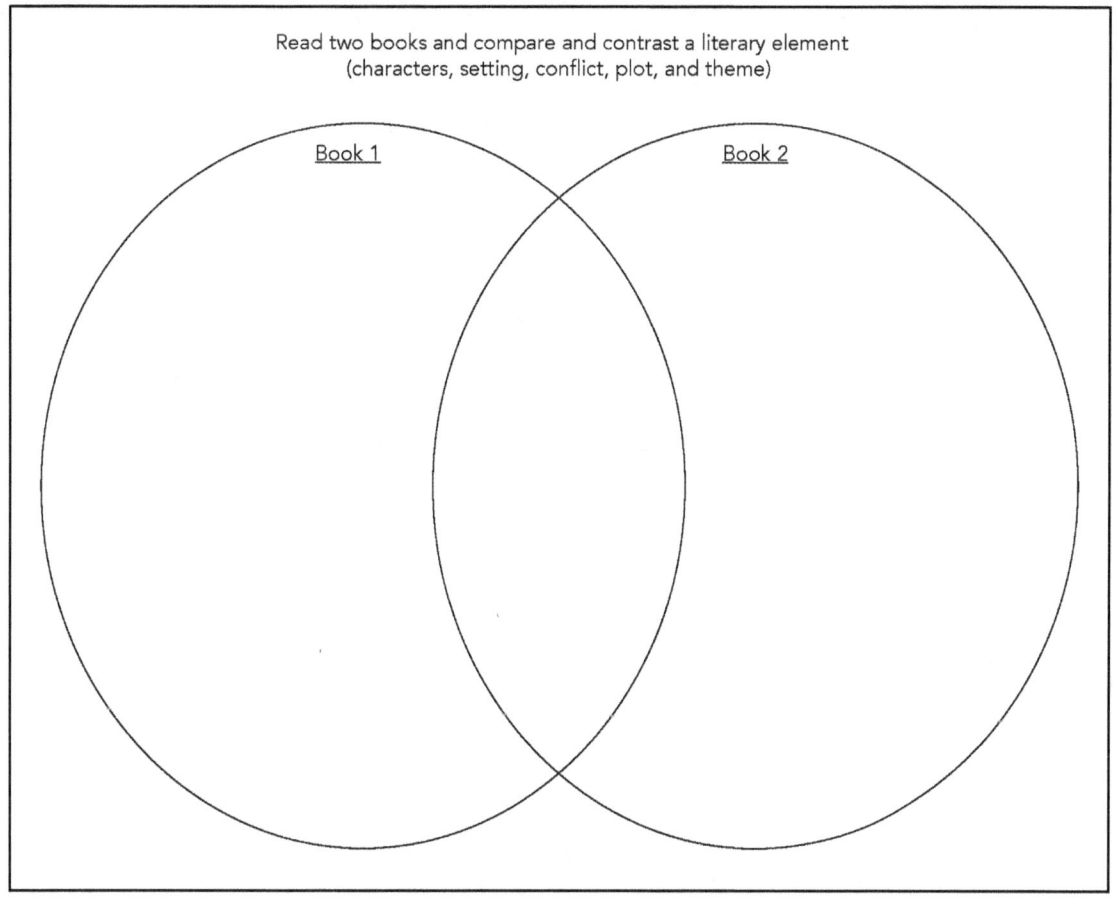

Read two books and compare and contrast a literary element
(characters, setting, conflict, plot, and theme)

Book 1   Book 2

Student booklets are available via the QR code at the end of the book

_____
Book Title

_____
Book Title

_____
Title of Book One

_____
Title of Book Two

Student booklets are available via the QR code at the end of the book

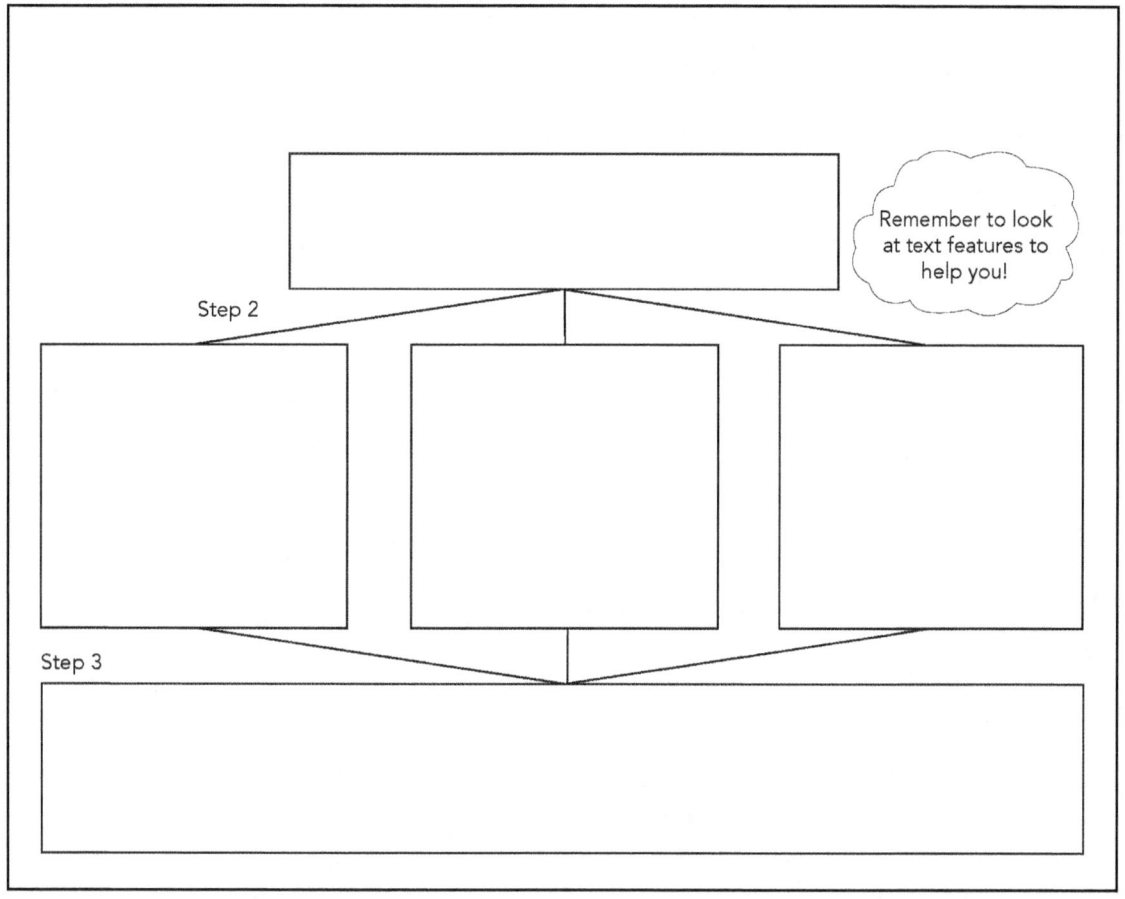

Step 2

Remember to look at text features to help you!

Step 3

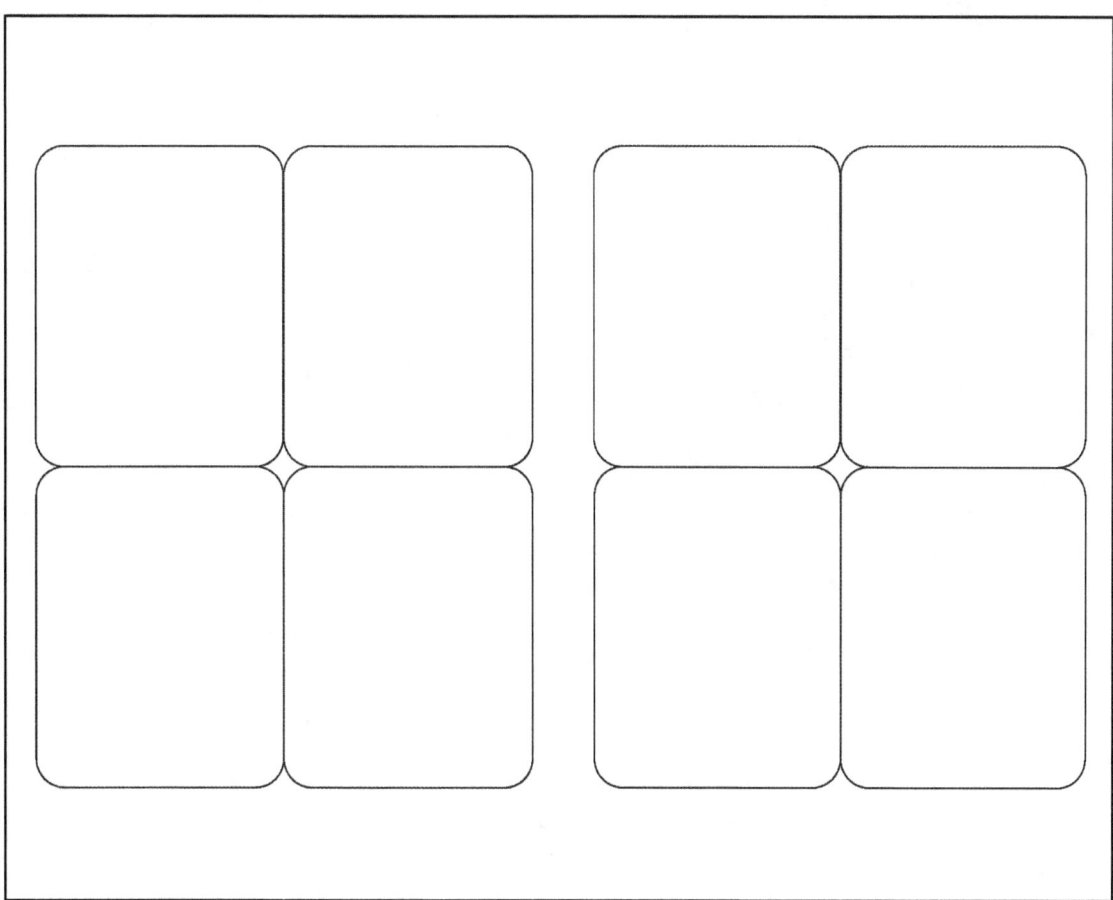

Student booklets are available via the QR code at the end of the book

STUDENT BOOKLET DOWNLOAD

Purchasers of **How to Create Language Experts with Literary Terms** may use this QR code to download booklets from this book at no extra cost. This will ease the process of making copies for students and expand learning options. Both the print and digital download versions of this material are protected by copyright laws.

QR codes can be found in all LtoJ books, providing access to digital downloads of student worksheets.

ABOUT THE AUTHORS

Codi Hrouda grew up in the small town of Hubbard, Nebraska. After completing high school, Codi went on to pursue her degree in Elementary Education at Wayne State College, and graduated with a BA in Elementary Education in 2000.

Once graduated, Codi accepted her first job at Thurston Elementary School, in Thurston, Nebraska, as a fifth and sixth grade combination teacher. A year later, she and her husband moved to Columbus, Nebraska where she taught a year of first grade and then thirteen years of fourth grade at Centennial Elementary School. While teaching full-time in Columbus, she completed her master's degree in Curriculum and Instruction through Wayne State College. She graduated with her master's degree in May of 2006.

In 2014, Codi and her husband moved their family back to the area where she grew up to raise their three daughters. Codi accepted a fifth grade position at Dakota City Elementary in Dakota City, Nebraska where she continues to teach today. She just completed her twenty-second year of teaching in 2022. Codi spends her free time attending her daughters' activities, decorating, reading, and spending time with her family and friends.

Emma McInerney grew up in the small town of Elk Point, South Dakota. After completing high school, Emma went on to pursue a degree in healthcare at South Dakota State University (SDSU).

In 2015, she realized she was ready for a career change because her passion lies in education. She transferred to Dakota State University (DSU), earned a degree in Elementary Education, and graduated in 2019. Emma began her first job at Dakota City Elementary, in Dakota City, Nebraska, as a fifth grade teacher. While teaching full-time she completed her Masters degree in Curriculum and Instruction through Wayne State College, graduating in May of 2022. Emma concluded her third year of teaching in 2022, and she continues to teach alongside her co-author, Codi Hrouda.

Emma returned to her hometown of Elk Point after graduating, and spends her free time reading, gardening, and spending time with her boyfriend, family, and friends.

Dr. Lyle Lee Jenkins is an author, speaker, and recognized authority in improving educational outcomes. He believes that implementing a growth mindset and celebrating progress are the keys to helping students learn more and retain their enthusiasm for school.

His education experience, that spans over 50 years, ranges from working as a teacher, a principal, and a school superintendent in the California School System to being a University Professor. In 2003, Lyle Lee founded LtoJ, LLC hoping to impact and guide the way we approach education.

Lyle Lee Jenkins has authored six books showcasing continuous improvement in schools, including *How to Create a Perfect School, Optimize Your School, Permission to Forget, From Systems Thinking to Systemic Action, Improving Student Learning,* and *How to Create a Perfect Home School.* All literature offers powerful, practical suggestions for every aspect of education. The two most influential people supporting Dr. Jenkins's work are W. Edwards Deming and John Hattie.

Having spoken to educators all across the United States, Latin America, Europe, Australia, and Asia, Lyle Lee Jenkins is passionate about equipping the next generation with a true love of learning.

Dr. Lyle Lee Jenkins holds a Bachelor of Arts degree from Point Loma Nazarene University, a Masters of Education from San Jose State University and a Ph.D. from the Claremont Graduate University.

Lyle Lee Jenkins's website, www.LtoJ.net, is a great place to discover useful tools to guide your educational journey.

Do you have a great photo or video of your student using one of our products?

We would love the opportunity to share it on our website and social media channels!

Email us at <u>info@ltoj.net</u>

If you have a story to share, we would also like to hear from you. We feature student stories during presentations and on our social media accounts.

Our team loves sharing the joy of a child understanding new concepts. It allows our audience to experience firsthand the mission our team works towards every day; for students to maintain the same love of learning they brought to Kindergarten throughout all their years of schooling and into adulthood.

Thank you for being a loyal customer. We appreciate you!

The LtoJ Team

Follow us on Instagram, Facebook, TikTok and YouTube
@LtoJLLC

www.ingramcontent.com/pod-product-compliance
Lightning Source LLC
Chambersburg PA
CBHW081010120626
46546CB00010B/3091